AIN'T NOTHING NICE

AIN'T NOTHING NICE

Veronica Junior-Hunter

Table of Contents

ACKNOWLEDGEMENTS.................................. 8

Some Days.. 9

Drive Time.. 10

When You Look Into My Eyes......................... 12

In This Poem I Can Brag.............................. 14

Who Am I... 15

You Are Doing Too Much............................. 17

You Got to Keep it Real.............................. 18

Tell Me Why My Guy Had to Die..................... 20

The First Time.. 22

The Map to a Woman................................... 23

The Niggas I Try to Avoid............................ 25

They Think You're Better Than Them............... 27

How Do You Know if I'm the One..................... 28

I Can be Your Everything............................. 30

My Man Kent... 32

Self-Worth.. 34

I'm Sorry.. 35

Cain... 37

Get Off... 38

Welfare Pimping... 39

Summer.. 41

I Remember When....................................... 42

My Cadillac (Past and Present)....................... 44

My Night at Savoy... 45

Love Jones Poetry Night................................ 47

Let Me Tell You a Little Bit About My Pimp........ 49

My Sista Locks... 51

Under Cover Friend.. 52

Untitled... 54

Thank You... 55

Sunshine... 57

Chase That Check.. 58

What It Means to Be at Work........................... 60

25/50.. 61

Thin Line... 63

Alabama Abortion Law.................................... 64

Street Dreams.. 67

Let's Make Love Tonight................................. 70

Have Anybody Seen My Man........................... 73

Raised in the Game.. 76

Charge It to the Game.................................... 80

Amusement Park of Life.................................. 82

DIVA... 84

Ghetto Bougie.. 86

Black & Gold.. 88

Ain't Nothing Nice.. 91

This Monster Called Cancer............................ 94

26 minutes.. 96

Bittersweet.. 97

*To my best friend and husband Kent.
Thanks for loving my child, mild and wild sides.*

ACKNOWLEDGEMENTS

I wrote my first poem at 8 years old. It was about my brother, James Junior. I also wrote a short song about him.

I have to thank my first friend for the inspiration. I can remember writing poems all the time, but I didn't know my words were important back then. I threw them all out with the trash. If I knew then, what I know now, I would have a catalog of poems. In 1990 I wrote the poem *I Can Be Your Everything* for someone special going through a trying time. I cherished that poem. In late 1997 I was going through a rough period. Dawn Hale encouraged me to recite my poem at Emerald City Love Jones Poetry Night. The first week I performed *I Can Be Your Everything* and received much love. The following week I reflected on my lifestyle and hardships and wrote *Ain't Nothing Nice* and brought the house down. That day I felt like a poet. Every week I wrote a new poem to perform on Tuesday Love Jones Poetry Night.

In the early 2000s I was introduced to the Mecca on Hampton. Dasha Kelly challenged poets to write poems on the spot to recite. Every Thursday the host would tell us what the word of the day would be, and we wrote a poem about that word. I thank Dasha often through prayers because she broadened my horizon. A few of my poems are not for the faint at heart. Some poems are low down, raw and scream Phoxxy. Using words or phrases I would never use in my poetry today. Some poems are fun-loving and match my Ronnie character as others are more mature or politically incorrect that flows with Veronica's nature.

SOME DAYS

Some days I'm joyful and is sublime

Some days there was hustling without a dime

Some days I wasted a lot of precious time

Some days I battled against the life of grime

Some days I willingly did the crime

Some days I got writers block and couldn't rhyme

Some days I thought I was reaching my prime

Some days I judge myself and felt like slime

Some days I waited for the ghetto bells to chime

Some days I'm in my imaginary box like a mime

Some days you'll know that I'm.......

DRIVE TIME

Tick Tock, Tick Tock, it's 5 O'clock, it's 5 O'clock,
It's time to unwind and unlock,
It's time to cruise the Ghetto blocks,
It's time to pop open the Private Stock.
IT'S RHYME TIME, PRIME TIME, IT'S JIVE TIME, DRIVE TIME

Rolling down the streets, while taking a blast,
Watching the children play, thinking about the past,
Reminiscing, about the crazy shit I did,
When I was a nappy-headed, snotty-nose kid.
IT'S RHYME TIME, PRIME TIME, IT'S JIVE TIME, DRIVE TIME

Riding and chilling, hitting all the hot spots,
Hollering at my guys gambling on the lots,
Telling them," to past the blunt around",
Ribbing on each other while holding my ground.
IT'S RHYME TIME, PRIME TIME, IT'S JIVE TIME, DRIVE TIME

After a long day at the job,
Hanging out drinking & getting high with the mob,
Thinking, I'm so happy with my life,
Drive time is over, got to get home to the wife.
IT'S RHYME TIME, PRIME TIME, IT'S JIVE TIME, DRIVE TIME

Laughing, to myself out loud,
Content with my world, feeling mighty proud,
We don't know, what tomorrow will bring,
I guarantee you; I'll be doing the same thing.
WAITING FOR RYHME TIME, PRIME TIME, WAITING FOR JIVE
TIME, DRIVE TIME

WHEN YOU LOOK IN MY EYES AND TELL ME LIES

In my 20s you was the man I idolized,

With your charming ways and good looks you mesmerized.

But even then you looked in my eyes and told me lies.

First of all I must admit I forgot I am the prize,

Because of the things you did between my thighs.

I acted unintelligent even though I am wise,

I let you get away with that good guy disguise.

Your honesty I continuously criticize,

You often look in my eyes and tell me lies.

Your many emotional relationships you don't recognize,

The 2, 3 or 4 other women you often denies.

Players in their 60s is on the rise,

Respecting my spirit you regularly defies,

And my mentality you readily chastise.

Out the window my ego flies,

My health and well-being you endlessly jeopardize,

While you look in my eyes and tell me lies.

I wanted more so in my heart I would improvise,

Many times all I asked was for you to compromise,

Because I was taken on many lows and a few highs.

You put me in the category with the mediocre punks and broke me down to their size,

All along looking in my eyes and telling me lies.

At this point I must realize,

For all you done to me you will never apologize.

And as the love between you and I dies,

It's just time to say our goodbyes.

IN THIS POEM I CAN BRAG

In this poem I can brag

In this poem I can also rag

On all those Negros who dare to sag

Their ass showing and perpetrating being a fag

In this poem I can brag

They hate on me and that's a drag

For reasons to make me want to gag

I'm never giving up by exposing my white flag

In this poem I can brag

When haters try to throw me a snag

Or portray me as a penniless hag

I shake it off because there's plenty of bread in my bag

In this poem I can brag

In this poem I can also nag

I don't start zigging when I want to zag

Don't put me down for having swag

You all know I come with a hefty price tag

In this poem I can brag

WHO AM I?

I am a wife, mother, sister, Maintenance Administrator and friend.

Being reliable, dependable and on the job every day I highly recommend.

I got the best job ever and I'm often told I'm clever.

I've been in Maintenance, Stare-Compare, Provisioning and DSL;

I've had many opportunities in this company to excel.

When asked to volunteer, I'm the first to raise my hand;

That's because I want my knowledge to expand.

Every employee here at the LOC is like a family member to me;

Sometimes we clash and have to agree to disagree.

I've celebrated many birthdays, marriages and bundles of joy;

We come together at Christmas to buy the tots a toy.

My family at the LOC had been there for me, and I've been there for them through sorrow and tears;

We've handled a lot in our 14 years.

My job is exciting, and I try to be a big help;

But some of the calls make me want to yelp.

Even though I love my position and I'm very content;

I'm still looking forward to an early retirement.

YOU ARE DOING TOO MUCH

YOU ARE DOING TOO MUCH!

YOU TRY TO CRIPPLE ME BUT I FOUND MY CRUTCH

YOU ARE DOING TOO MUCH!

BEING CARELESS, IMPULSIVE, WILD AND SUCH

YOU ARE DOING TOO MUCH!

THINKING AT ALL TIMES YOU HAVE THE MIDAS TOUCH

YOU ARE DOING TOO MUCH!

YOU ASKED HER FOR A DATE SHE FINDS OUT SHE IS GOING
DUTCH

YOU ARE DOING TOO MUCH!

SLOW GRINDING AT THE QUARTER PARTY
BROKE GRANDMA'S HUTCH

YOU ARE DOING TOO MUCH!

BAILED YOUR BROKE ASS OUT WHEN YOU WERE IN A
CLUTCH

YOU ARE DOING TOO MUCH!!!!

YOU GOT TO KEEP IT REAL

You got to keep it real!
Can you keep it real?
You must keep it real!
You got to keep it real!
Your shoes are hard to fill,
When you're keeping it real.
You got to climb that high hill,
Are you keeping it real?
I don't have any time to kill.
I'm trying to keep it real!
In your head I must drill,
Just keep it real!
Keeping it real,
Don't come in a pill.
You got to keep it real!
You got to keep it real!
Can you keep it real?
You must keep it real!
You got to keep it real!
If you're out of order then you got to chill,
And keep it real!
What is the big deal?

This is just how I feel.
I got to keep it real!
I am Phoxxy and I have sex appeal,
I'm just keeping real!
Just like the spike on my high heel,
I'm just keeping it real!
A kiss on your lips I'll seal,
Off your clothes I will peel.
Then my wildness I will reveal,
On my knees I might just kneel!
Did you know my favorite color is teal?
I'm just keeping it real.
Your thrills I fulfill,
When you're keeping it real.
You got to keep it real!
Can you keep it real?
You must keep it real!
You got to keep it real!
You got to keep it real!
You got to keep it real!
You got to keep it real!!!!!!!!

TELL ME WHY MY GUY HAD TO DIE

One day in July, he and I, getting high, smoking on that tye, I ain't gonna lie.
So here comes this wise guy, high, on that rye, hollering out a war cry.
He didn't specify, this tsetse fly, trying to signify.
Thinking his ego can multiply, when we all know he's only a small fry.
I didn't want to pry, I asked my baby why, this passerby, popped Vi, in the eye.
My guy, wanting to rectify, what was going on his reply, was Vi, can rely, on him to satisfy, the situation. Mud pie, defy, to comply, with his suggestion to see eye to eye.
Dude aura began to intensify, because he couldn't identify, with the fact that my guy, was there just to pacify.
I have to clarify, that I, classify, him as a hero.
My guy, wasn't gun shy, and didn't think this Pigsty, had such an evil eye,
And made it come down to do or die.
POW!! POW!! POW!! POW!! POW!! POW!!
I was on standby; because I didn't get a chance to tell him beddy-bye.
It did horrify me when I heard him glorify what he done.
What he did they won't verify, what I said don't apply, and what you seen don't qualify.

Your statements they can falsify, when they unify, these people we call the FBI.
They will crucify, at a blink of an eye, and certify, that they have an alibi.
Then it's a whole different story when they testify, and any wrong doing you know they'll justify.
I used to cry, and try, to deny, what this ally, did to my cutie-pie.
So now I'm left high and dry, so tell me why, my, guy, had to die, before I got a chance to say goodbye.

THE FIRST TIME

TRYING TO REMEMBER ALL THE STUFF I DID, WHEN I WAS A KID.

THE FIRST TIME I MADE LOVE, WE FIT TOGETHER LIKE A HAND IN A GLOVE.

THINKING BACK AFAR, THE FIRST TIME I DROVE A CAR.

AND THE FIRST TIME I WENT INTO A BAR.
BEING A TEENAGER AND ALL, BUT I THOUGHT I WAS A STAR
.
THE FIRST TIME I SAW MY BABY'S FACE AND I KNEW RIGHT AWAY SHE WAS MINE.
EVEN THOUGHT I WAS YOUNG I FIGURED OUR LIFE WOULD BE JUST FINE.

THE FIRST TIME I HEARD MY BABY BOY CRY.
THAT WAS THE SWEETEST SOUND I EVER HEARD, I'M NOT GONNA LIE.
THE FIRST TIME I REALIZED BEFORE I LET ANYTHING HAPPEN TO MY TWO BEAUTIFUL CHILDEN I WOULD DIE.

THE MAP TO A WOMAN

Girlfriends you must be brassy,
Learn the difference between trashy and classy,
And have a personality that sexy yet sassy.

You know men sometimes we may think you attitude is defective,
We might think your rap is ineffective,
Because some of us women are a little selective.
You'll just have to be objective,
And put your shit in the proper prospective.

Now suppose you spot a honey that's vivacious,
Beautiful in every way and curvaceous.
Not too much, but be a little flirtatious,
And make her feel by being in the presence you're gracious.

We want you to be like Crystal Blue Persuasion,
Fly gear, down, prepared for any occasion.

Your attention is what we want to captivate,
Our intelligence we want you to stimulate,
And our mental, emotional, sexual and financial needs you should
want to accommodate.

We need you to be very nonchalant,
Be our main confidante and take us to some of the fanciest
restaurants,
These are just a few little things we as ladies want.

Chivalry, class and sex appeal is what we pleasure,
With a talk so deep giving us multiple mental orgasms we can't measure,
OK fellas, I've given you the map it's up to you to find the treasure.

THE NIGGAS I TRY TO AVOID

In people's business you always probe,
Heavy artillery is part of your wardrobe.
Stealing from anyone including your kinfolk,
Take nothing serious; thinks life's a joke.
All you want from me is my money and my spokes,
You see, the attitude I have you provokes.
Don't you understand that I get annoyed,
By you niggas I try to avoid.

To one woman you can never be loyal,
Everybody's life you become involved with turns to turmoil,
Any goodness that comes along you're sure to foil,
OOh, y'all just make my temperature boil.
Your way of thinking, STRAIGHT UP, make me paranoid,
You niggas I try to avoid.

Never went to school, don't even have a G.E.D.,
Think you're doing good living off your Ghetto Degree.
If a gang comes along you're the first one to join,
Walking down the street holding on to your groin,
With nothing in your pocket not even one coin.
If you're living a life too scandalous for the tabloids,
Then you are the niggas I try to avoid.

Bragging about what you did to get on parole,
In life never set an honest goal.
Can't give a female your mind, body or soul,
Don't see a woman as your equal or as a whole.
Your temperament is beyond your control,
Complains you don't want to be on the white man's payroll.

Geek monster, prisoner of the system or one that chooses to be broke or unemployed,
Because you don't pay child support your children's dreams are destroyed,
Knowing without money their lives can never be fully enjoyed.
Yes, YOU are the niggas I try to avoid.

THEY THINK YOU'RE BETTER THAN THEM

They'll dis you and dismiss you, because they wish you, wasn't
better than them;

They'll jive you, try to connive you, then deprive you, they think
you're better than them;

They'll entice you and sacrifice you, at any price you
are better than them;

They'll depress you, and try to stress you,
then confess, you are better than them;

They'll dread you and try to shred you,
they even said, you are better than them;

They'll frustrate you and aggravate you,
then demonstrate, you are better than them;

They'll try to scam you, hey ma'am--- you know,
you're better than them;

They'll try to blame you and even frame you,
they're ashamed, you are better than them;

They'll use you, and abuse you, then accuse you,
of being better than them;

When they praise you, it will amaze you,
It's them that portray you, as being better than them.

HOW DO YOU KNOW IF I'M THE ONE

When you're with me you feel as if you've just won the lottery.
Our love sessions so intense make your eyes watery.

You're constantly thinking is this live or Memorex,
Or is it only our bodies, not our minds that connects.
I'm everything you want in a woman you suspect.

HOW DO YOU KNOW IF I'M THE ONE

Are you in a trance,
Wondering if a true romance,
Will advance.

You realize I'm all you need from this day forward,
Thinking, to be without me would be absurd.

You don't want to play love games in which you don't have the rules,
Or you don't want to leave me hanging like a fool.
And you value what we have as if it was precious jewels.

HOW DO YOU KNOW IF I'M THE ONE

You'll know you got my front and sides covered and I got your back.
Thinking this thing we got going is on the right track,
Confidently together big dollars we'll stack.

You now have someone you can call your honey, dear or boo,
You feel like screaming out baby, I LOVE YOU!!!

You're wondering where I have been all of your life,
Knowing I possess the qualities of a good wife.

HOW DO YOUR KNOW IF I'M THE ONE

Afraid of the feeling you nervously shake,
You're wondering is this fake,
In your mind a mistake?
I say you may now make your break,
Which will later prevent the heartache.
Or stand there thinking today, "What a beautiful bride I'll make?

YOU NOW KNOW I AM THE ONE.

I CAN BE YOUR EVERYTHING

I can be your everything if given the chance, all I need is your time,
love, kindness and romance.

I can be the perfect mother to your child and do all that freaky shit to
drive you wild.

I can be your baker and bake you tarts, cakes and pies,
You will never have to worry about dishonesty, disloyalty or lies.

I can be your doctor and keep you well from head to feet,
Hey baby, this thing we're going through we'll have to defeat.

I CAN BE YOUR EVERYTHING; I CAN BE YOUR EVERYTHING

I can be your everything and dance so exotic,
Then be there for you when you're feeling erotic.

I can be your everything because I know you're about big money,
I know deep inside you do what you got to do honey.

I can be your everything it's for you to discover,
I put my all in everything not just being a good lover.

I can be your everything eventually your wife,
But for now I'm just hoping and praying that we'll be together for life.

I CAN BE YOUR EVERYTHING; I CAN BE YOUR EVERYTHING

I can be your everything because I love you a lot,
Yes, baby you know where all the right spots.

I can be your everything I hope we'll never part,
I wrote this for you, and it came straight from my heart.

I can be your everything I can even be your proxy,
I know exactly what to do to keep you happy that's why they call me
PHOXXY.

My Man Kent

Many men have come and went

His positive influence in my life is evident

The coldest man in Milwaukee and such a handsome gent

Not saying he's an angel but he was heaven sent

My Man Kent

He promised to take care of my bills and my rent

Every day I receive a compliment

He excuses my temperament

Blowing thousands on me and feels it's well spent

Every morning I am content

When I wake up next to My Man Kent

When he thinks of his future I am his main component

No questions asked he would never leave me a bent

And has a life plan we can both implement

He's my soul mate and that's keeping it 100 percent

To write this poem that portrays this sentiment

And express the love I have for My Man Kent

To seek out my King was my intent

Our connection is stronger than cement

With my body he loves to experiment

In this glorified moment

I am shouting out to the world I am going to represent

This beautiful relationship I have with My Man Kent

SELF WORTH

In my imagination far and beyond
I thought what we had was a close bond
It was only me that was conned
Before I even got a chance to respond

He's been playing with my mind for so long
He made me weak when I use to be strong
I could be right he tells me I'm wrong
I know he's my biggest problem all along

I think my life is just an illusion
Now that I've come to the conclusion
That my world is full of confusion

In my mind I can't compute
Your evil ways you can't dispute
You blindly lead me to the forbidden fruit
Now you want to prosecute
Or make me feel I'm in an institute

Don't you understand honesty is a must
I now know you I cannot trust
You just make me feel disgust
It's more than your attitude you'll have to adjust

Now I removed the girth
It's my sanity I rebirth
So why on earth
Would I let him determine my self-worth

I'M SORRY

I'm sorry for not being the man you thought I should be
I'm sorry for trying to throw down that player shit from 1973

I'm sorry for lying about my other bitches
I'm sorry for thinking about pussy and not the riches

I'm sorry for hurting your heart to the core
I'm sorry for using you as a score

I'm sorry for taking your love for granted
I'm sorry for being admired by you and now you're disenchanted

I'm sorry for making you feel less then
I'm sorry for lying about you to the other women

I'm sorry for not following your program
I'm sorry for falling for any and every scam

I'm sorry for not making you my priority
I'm sorry for not choosing you over my sorority

I'm sorry for stumbling over thousands to get to a penny
I'm sorry for putting others before you and yes there were many

I'm sorry for doing it to you again and not loving you till the end
I'm sorry for not having your back and not being a good friend

I'm sorry for my narcissist and selfishness
I'm sorry for all I've done wrong to you I must confess

I'm sorry for dimming your light so mine can shine bright
I'm sorry for making you feel you were in twilight

I'm sorry for thinking I was slick and trying to be cool
I'm sorry for being a stupid, low down sorry ass fool

I'm sorry for being a bloodsucker
I'm sorry for being a lousy mother fucker

CAIN

Cain can hit you harder than a train
Make you feel like you've been sprayed with acid rain
You'll feel like your life is in a hurricane
Make your heart race faster than a jet plane
Cain is very inhumane
Make you do anything for that hit, that drain
Or that shot in the vein
Crawling on the floor trying to get every grain
Cain will make it hard for you to restrain
Your money will take a walk down memory lane
On your family you'll put a big strain
Cain don't care who you slain
Make you feel like you're going insane
You know that shit will fry your brain
So if you know like I know, you'll try to abstain
Let me explain
I'm not here to complain
My composure I'm just trying to maintain
And let's get together and start a campaign
Not to let Cocaine in our domain
And I'll toast you sipping on my champagne
CAIN WILL GIVE YOU PAIN NO GAIN

GET-OFF

I just want to take a hit and blast-off

Sitting back waiting on that lift-off

I tried to get-off

But I got cut-off

As he gave me the brush-off

It will be a big kick-off

And a rip-off

Without a pay-off

I'll get-off

Due to being well-off

I can't take the trade-off

Of being a show-off

GET OFF

WELFARE PIMPING

He's just a Welfare Pimp

He only get paid once a month

Tell me girl, what you gonna do

He's waiting on the mailman harder than you

He's standing in line at the bank

Out your hands the money he yanks

Perpetrating in front of his friends

Don't you know the fake shit about to end

He's Welfare Pimping you

Tell me girl what is he gonna do

When the state starts W-2

Welfare Pimping always made kids suffer

But W-2 is gonna make it rougher

Life will be tougher

So Sisters get off your asses and don't be lazy

And Brothers don't let this situation drive you crazy

Take good care of the kids my friend

Because Welfare Pimping coming to an end

You'll have to put him in Welfare Pimping pasture, I figure

Along with all the other Welfare Pimping niggers

So come on ladies with or without a man

Make the best of the shit anyway you can

Get a grip on reality and make a plan

WHAT YOU GONNA DO; WHEN THE STATE STARTS W-2

SUMMER

Summer sun shining bright in my face

Yellowness surrounding the space

The smell of warmth is in the air

The leaves are blowing without a care

Listening to the birds singing so sweet

As the clouds retreat

The grass freshly cut

A squirrel securing his chestnut

The flowers blooming

And the insects zooming

The sounds of children laughter

Enjoying the summer hereafter

I REMEMBER WHEN

I remember when we got up and changed the channels
Everybody and their momma's had wood panels.

I remember the carpet was shaggy
We wore skin tights we wouldn't be caught dead in clothes that were baggy.

I remember when we use to do the Camel Walk, Break Down, Push-N-Pull, Funky Chicken, Penguin, Electric Guitar the list goes on and on
I even remember when we didn't have 911.

I remember when my grandma used to go out decked in her sequins, diamonds and fur
Thinking when I get grown I going to be just like her.

I remember when the Cable Company was Select
And everybody gave his or her elders the utmost respect.

I remember when we use to trick or treat at night
Mom not worrying knowing every thing's going to be alright.

I remember when my mother tried to tell me right from wrong
I also remember not listening because I was too headstrong.

I remember the CB's in every other car or customized van
And one of my favorite games was Pac-Man.

I remember how funny brothas looked in their Psychedelic shirts,
high waist pants and 4-inch stacks
Styling with their white walls on their big Cadillac.

I remember when groovy, right on, soul power and I'm hip was the
perfect phrase

YES, THOSE WERE THE GOOD OLD DAYS

MY CADILLAC (PAST AND PRESENT)

Styling in my teal Cadillac
Woofers bumping loud in the back
Looking better than a KFC 3 piece snack

Driving my black and grey Cadillac
Rolling down the street on the right track
Not listening to the players talks their smack

Sitting in my mauve Cadillac
Slick behind the wheel with paper in the sack
Being dubbed the queen of the pack

Chilling in my red Cadillac
A black belt and always ready for the attack
Telling me I'm the female version of a Mack

Succeeding in my blue Cadillac
Leaning on my dreams that didn't crack
Have someone that got my back and takes up the slack

Profiling in my white Cadillac
Don't have time for the crap that's whack
Those millions I will continue to stack
With one on the best stamped on my plaque

Yes, I love my Cadillacs!

MY NIGHT AT SAVOY

Let me tell you this story and I swear it's true.
Shit like this don't happen every day to me or you.

I went to this hot spot called SAVOY.
With a half-smile on my face and being very coy.
Just the feeling of the night brought me joy.

When I first stepped in, the champagne started flowing.
I was looking good and radiantly glowing.

As I walked through the club all eyes were on me,
To get a glimpse, I should have been charging a fee.

I had on a tight leather suit, short skirt hugging my hips,
Thigh high suede boots with pointy toe tips.

Oozing with sex appeal and seeping with class,
The opportunity to show it off I couldn't pass.
So I got on the dance floor, started shaking my ass, shaking my ass.

Popping it and jerking it, as if I was on stage,
Doing it like at the end of the dance, I was getting a wage.

Apparently I caught this fly guy eye,
To get a chance to rap to me he couldn't pass it by.

He introduce himself to me as Stan,
Right away I had a notion that he is THE MAN.

He offered me a drink and tickets to a play,
All I could think about is today has been a good day.

He had on a jazzy silk shirt, Louis Vuitton boots
Jewels bling, bling, like he's all about his loot.

After buying me a few drinks, conversation stimulating,
A very strong interest in me he's indicating.
His every word sounding so fascinating,
His mature look and style, captivating.

As long as I live, forever will this memory linger,
He pulled out a ring told me to put it on my finger.
Checking it out it's a magnificent, beautiful 1-carat of a humdinger.

I try to be nonchalant and laid back as a rule,
As excited as I was, I maintain my cool.
The rock so damn big makes you want to drool.

Looked up, thanked God, because I know I'm blessed.
To this man I confessed,
To the utmost I am impressed.

If nothing come this but just mere friends,
I will never forget that night at Savoy's until my life ends

LOVE JONES POETRY NIGHT

All I wanted was your attention,

Because I have some shit that I must mention.

Let's just see what disrespect person is going to talk though this poem,

Look that sap sucker straight in the eye and tell him to go home.

That you came here as I did to listen to these creative writers,

Because Love Jones Poetry Nights make my days a little brighter.

If sitting back chilling with your mouth closed isn't what you like,

Go to Victor's, Andre's or Junior's take your ass a hike.

Everyone in here is 21 and up,

Be mature and I toast you, lifting my cup.

We shouldn't have to shhh you, because, your ass is grown,

Just remove yourself from the situation and leave us alone.

When I first started reading my poems here, you were feeling me and I was feeling y'all,

After the readings was the dancing and I be having a ball.

Emerald city is a place where I can express myself on a Wednesday night,

And my poems every week have been tight.

But you just have to listen to my words alright.

Oh, my poems and raps are deep,

They contain experiences and knowledge that you might want to keep.

So just be quiet and listen we say,

When you get up here close attention I'll pay.

LET ME TELL YOU A LITTLE BIT ABOUT MY PIMP

He wakes me every morning, talking about he's hungry.

You know what I do?

Get up and fix him breakfast.

Because that's when he's at his very best.

I have to wash his draws, shirts and socks;

I do it because he's so fine with his curly locks.

Ponytail hanging down his back;

Every female idea of a Mack.

He's a very sharp dresser, I buy his clothes;

And that's a fact everybody knows.

His shoes a hundred dollars a pop; jeweled down;

And he loves to get chauffeured around town.

He asks me for money every single day;

I give it to him because that's the price I have to pay.

Because when he come to me and say;

"Mommy I made the honor roll",

"Mommy I love you with all my heart and soul",

"Mommy I got all A's again",

"For you mom, certificates and Karate Trophies I'll win".

When he looks at me with those big brown I melt,

Ain't that a blimp;

Let me tell you a little bit about my pimp.

My Sista Locks

When I first got my hair locked

I was shocked

Loving natural hair my mind blocked

And I knew I was going to get mocked

Everyone calls me the Phox

I now love my long golden Sista locks

Big money my Loctician Symone clocks

The cost is just the school of hard knocks

So expensive I need to buy stocks

Because we're a team that rocks

After 9 years still loving my Sista Locks

UNDER COVER FRIEND

Portraying to be my best friend
With the jealous vibes you send

My man takes us out and treats us like a queen
Thinking this love you can come between
Under cover friend is on the scene

I provided you with all my hot spots
To steal my life you plots

Is she really my friend or foe
Can she really dive that low
Under cover friend you must go

Blessed I got this far unscathed
Surprised by the way they behaved

What you're putting down is a shame
You haven't changed it's all the same
Under cover friend remaining lame

Dedication upon you I had bestowed
My trust you didn't hold

Whispers of forever more
Game so tight no need to keep score
Under cover friend I'll always be the one you adore

To give you my heart I didn't hesitate
My kindness you couldn't appreciate

What we had we thought wouldn't bend
We let the bull crap make the relationship end
You're dismissed my under cover friend

God has given me the gift of words it's a sin not to share
My words are copy written so steal them if you dare

My poems are tight and that's a known fact
Keeping my poisonous pen intact
Under cover fake friend you're caught in the act

UNTITLED

I'm strong in everything that I do
I'm broken down and weak when it comes to you

I'm discipline and stand by my convictions
And will add you to the list of my addictions

I have to admit you are my real first true love
My sincere affections you are unworthy of

I'm dedicated and proved I'm deserving
You are not I'm constantly observing

Honesty is important I have stressed that many times
Dismissing your faults and your long record of crimes

I strived for excellence throughout the years
Things you have done has brought me to tears

I try to stay faithful and stand by your side
You have figured out ways to make me eat my pride

I stay focus and bank on that cash flow
You tricks off and assumes I have thousands to blow

I was obsessed and you used to keep me amused
Now you often leave me bewildered and confused

The relationship we have is somewhat sick
Love making so good makes me a crazed lunatic

Knowing you have lips of flame and a heart of stone
One day I may get the strength to leave you alone

THANK YOU

THANK YOU DIANE & JAMES FOR CREATING ME

THANK YOU HAZEL HORTON FOR MOLDING ME

THANK YOU ANNIE JUNIOR FOR NURTURING

THANK YOU OTIS JUNIOR FOR CULTIVATION ME

THANK YOU BERNICE JUNIOR FOR STIMULATING ME

THANK YOU JUDY JUNIOR FOR EDUCATING ME

THANK YOU OLLIE-PAT-SHIRLEY FOR ENLIGHTENING ME

THANK YOU JAMES JUNIOR FOR BROTHERING ME

THANK YOU TONI JUNIOR FOR SISTERING ME

THANK YOU ALISHA JORDAN FOR ADMIRING ME

THANK YOU DUSTIN BOYD FOR CHALLENGING ME

THANK YOU MONTE JUNIOR FOR CRAFTING ME

THANK YOU MICHELLE JOY FOR BEFRIENDING ME

THANK YOU STEVE JUNIOR FOR AMUSING ME

THANK YOU COUSINS FOR VALIDATING ME

THANK YOU OLIVIA SMITH FOR SUPPORTING ME

THANK YOU DAWN HALE FOR FACILITATING ME

THANK YOU STERLING DANIELS, WANDA BAYLIS AND DOUG REYNOLDS FOR ENCOURAGING ME

THANK YOU DASHA AT THE MECCA FOR ENERGIZING ME

THANK YOU MICHAEL ARMON FOR MOTIVATING ME

THANK YOU TONY HARRIS FOR ENDORSING ME

THANK YOU AT&T FOR EMPLOYING ME

THANK YOU FAMILY AND FRIENDS FOR BACKING ME

THANK YOU NIKKI HUNTER FOR COVERING ME

THANK YOU CRAIG BROWN FOR ORGANIZING ME

THANK YOU KENT HUNTER FOR INSPIRING ME CHERISHING ME-LOVING ME-VALUING ME

THANKYOU!!!!!!!!!!!!!

SUNSHINE

Sitting here daydreaming in the sunshine.

My life and my world I'm trying to design.

The meaning of happiness I want to define.

Relaxing in the delightful sunshine.

Being straight forward and to the point is the bottom line.

Truth, peace, love and money is all mine.

As I chill here sipping my wine.

In this beautiful sunshine.

Must we not forget my man that tall, fit and fine.

Always wanting me, loving me and taking me to dine.

It is truly divine.

In the serene sunshine.

CHASE THAT CHECK

He gets up early before the sun rises
Knowing today is full of many surprises

Ready to hit the deck
It's time for him to chase that check

I make sure he's fed and dressed
I feel my days with him are blessed

Before leaving the house he gives me a peck
As he go chase that check

He says he thinks of me all day and night
Moments with him is pure delight

Sitting here chilling and thinking what the heck
While he chase that check

This man I love him so much and I owe him my life
Everyone knows he calls me "Wife"

He an excellent Central Office Tech
For me he happily chase that check

Still throwing it down hard at 67
Making me feel like I'm in heaven

No need to be a nervous wreck
He has my back and loves chasing that check

He takes me out most Friday's for a romantic date
I will love him forever he's my soul mate

Soon as he gets home my arms are around his neck
Dedicated to AT&T for 50 years chasing that check

WHAT IT MEANS TO BE AT WORK

When waking in the morning all tired and bent,
Don't grab that phone and call in sick, you'll be marked absent.

If I'm weary and at my end wits,
All I think of is SBC good benefits.

Employment I've had in the past,
Were funky dead end jobs that just didn't last.

I'm one to listen to what my managers say,
I strive to be a work every single day.

I don't want this building to shut down in a flash,
Because at the end of two weeks I want all my cash.

It brings me such a joy to sign in on time,
Compared to other employers SBC is prime.

We should all try our best to be here,
The end results will be 45 grand a year.

My morale is high and the workplace been great,
So I must send a special thanks to Kate.

To all my co-workers, friends and family don't be a jerk,
And prove what it means to us to be at work.

25 / 50

At 25 I knew everything; you could not tell me I was wrong
At 50 I want to learn something new every day; and still looks good in a thong

At 25 possibly a little shady, slick and would beat you down for the crown
At 50 I'm so laid back I don't have time to clown

At 25 I didn't admit to my mistakes and I did things Illegal, immoral or perhaps impractical
At 50 with my finances and my life skills I'm very tactical

At 25 I stared trouble in the face was involved with a lot of riff raff
At 50 after looking back and realizing how bold I was always makes me laugh

At 25 I went by Phoxxy travelled a few States and wanted to be internationally known
At 50 I'm therefore grateful and blessed to have reached this milestone

At 25 I was hot headed and flying high without leaving the ground
At 50 I jumped out of an airplane, and promises to never do that again, I am staying earthbound

At 25 I was broke, so I charged it to the game
At 50 my credit goes a long way and I'm proud of the woman I've became

At 25 around 11 or 12 I started getting ready for the night life
At 50 I'm leaving the party at that time to go home to be a good wife

At 25 I was looking forward to my 1st million and wanted to be filthy rich
At 50 I've established what's really important, a wonderful hubby, family, true friends, good health, I found my niche

At 25 no care in the world, all night long, I could drop it like it's hot, drop it like it's hot
At 50 I can still drop it like it's hot, getting old I am not

At 25 I didn't know what 50 looked like, you see
At 50 I now understand it took that 25 year old to be the best Mrs. Hunter I can be

THIN LINE

There's a thin line between a player and a trick

Nigga always thinks he's slick

Because he has a long fat dick

That's harder than a brick

And master the pussy he lick

There's a thin line between a player and a trick

Good loving never makes it quick

Has a good woman but gets down with any chick

Not getting paid makes me confoundedly sick

Dealing with punk bitches that run in a click

There's a thin line between a player and a trick

Laying down that magic stick

On pretty thick

Lying about she's your cousin, niece or sidekick

Needing to find out what makes you tick

There's a thin line between a player and a trick

It's your decision on which one your ass pick

ALABAMA ABORTION LAW

IF YOU GET MOLESTED IN ALABAMA NO ABORTION FOR RAPE

DUE TO ALL THE OLD WHITE MEN RED TAPE

YOU'LL JUST BE PREGNANT WITH YOUR RAPIST BABY

THEY SAY WITH THERAPY YOU'LL BE OK "MAYBE"

YOU HAD A LOVE AFFAIR WITH YOUR BROTHER

SICKNESS IS THE REASON THERE'S NO OTHER

YOU HAVE NO CHOICE BUT TO CARRY HIS CHILD

THE GOVERNMENT TELLING A WOMAN WHAT TO DO WITH HER BODY IS WILD

THE FETUS IS DEFORMED WITHOUT A HEAD

NO NEGOTIATIONS THE ABORTION CONVERSATION IS DEAD

YOU MUST GO THROUGH THIS UNTIL THE BABY'S FULL TERM

THEY WILL SEND THIS TO THE SUPREME COURT FOR THEM TO AFFIRM

THERE'RE TRYING TO THROW SHADE

BY OVERTURNING ROE VS WADE

ROE IS KNOWN WHERE ABORTIONS NATIONWIDE IS LEGALIZED

AND YOUR CONSTITUTIONAL RIGHT TO PRIVACY IS RECOGNIZED

THE US SUPREME COURT RULED IN JANUARY OF 1973

THAT EVERY WOMAN DECISION FOR CHOICE IS FREE

LEGALLY THE ABORTING DOCTOR WILL DO MORE TIME

THEN THE RAPIST THAT DID THE CRIME

ALABAMA'S BAN ON ABORTIONS WITH NO EXCEPTIONS

WITH THEIR LIES IN TRUST AND PLANNED OUT DECEPTIONS

YOU WILL NEVER UNDERSTAND THE RANGE OF MY ANGER

ABORTION IS AGAINST THE LAW UNLESS A MOTHER'S HEALTH IS IN DANGER

MISSOURI, OHIO AND GEORGIA IS TRYING TO DO THE SAME

GEORGIA HAS A "HEARTBEAT" LAW THAT'S LAME

MISSOURI IS TRYING TO CLOSE IT'S ONE AND ONLY PLANNED PARENTHOOD

THIS WILL CAUSE FEMALES LOOKING FOR MEDICAL ATTENTION NO GOOD

I DON'T WANT TO COME OFF AS BEING BRASS AND INDIGNANT

GOV KAY IVEY SIGNED THE ABORTION BAN BECAUSE SHE'S TO OLD TO GET PREGNANT

IN A LAND WHERE I WORK HARD AND MY MONEY IS SPENT

I HAVE THE RIGHT TO HAVE AN ABORTION WITHOUT UNDUE RESTRICTIVE INTERFERENCE FROM THE GOVERNMENT

STREET DREAMS

Thinking to myself, so far so good,
Keeping it real I'm often misunderstood.
I got a nice house on a hill in the hood,
They compare my crib to those in Hollywood.

I'm going forward and to the extreme,
Living the Street Dream, The Ghetto Street Dream.

I do my 8 hours on the job every day,
Then I put my hustle down to get more pay.
A couple of slick cars in my driveway,
Living large in the US of A.

As predictable as it may seem,
I'm living the Street Dream, The Ghetto Street Dream.

Sitting here spilling it I must be frank,
Every day I awake; it's the Lord I thank.
I got cash in my pockets, some in the bank,
I get what I want when I want it point-blank.

This rap right here, have a theme,
It's about living the Street Dream, The Ghetto Street Dream.

It took 3 years, now I'm out of debt,
With a pen & pad I know I'll be a threat.
I have only one regret,
I haven't made my 1st million yet.

I'm really into this regime,
And I'm living the Street Dream, The Ghetto Street Dream.

To never work for the white man he swore,
Folks describe him as being hard core.
On the comer always trying to score,
The battle he fights, worse than the cold-war.

Even when he's napping, he's wondering who he'll scheme,
He's living the Street Dream, The Ghetto Street Dream.

She got 5 babies, no job, says society to blame,
All different daddies, ain't that a damn shame.
The last man she had promised her fame,
All along it was just a game.

She's stressed-out and wants to scream,
Cause she's living the Street Dream, The Ghetto Street Dream.

Run the streets all day and night,
Always looking for a dirty fight.
At the end of the tunnel, he'll never see light,
But in his mind, everything's all right.

He know he'll never make the elite team,
He's living the Street Dream, The Ghetto Street Dream.

She's been giving him her love for the last 5 years,
Wasting all her precious time brings her to tears.
Wanting to have him to herself, thinking; maybe?
But then his wife had just given birth to their 2nd baby.

Her honor and respect she must redeem,
She's living the Street Dream, Ghetto Street Dream.

He get his cash flow anyway he can,
Loud talking and flexing to prove he's the man.
He can't respect the other guy's view,
If you disagree with him, he might do you.

As predictable as it may seem,
He's living the Street Dream, The Ghetto Street Dream.

LET'S MAKE LOVE TONIGHT

This gorgeous man walked thru the door;
I stared hard, need I say more.

The man's so jazzy, suave and intense;
the way I wanted him, made no sense.

My name and 7 digits he insisted;
with his look and charms, I couldn't resist it.

He called me on the telephone;
to ask me was the feeling on,
and did I want to be with him or alone.

Then he started singing:
Ahh. Let's make love tonight,
I'll take you on a love flight,
I'll make it feel alright.

Now, wait a minute, I have so much love to give.
But baby, it has to be real.

You know what's on my mind;
and you know I'm not the kind.

That would give my love away to a stranger;
I would never put my love in danger.

I must understand what you have planned.

Because I don't want this act of love to end in a one night stand.

Then he started singing again:
Ahh, Let's make love tonight,
I' ll take you to a height.
With me your future is bright.

O.K., Now, the decision I make. I must make it wisely;

Fuck it, turn on the box, because the PHOX is ready to make love to
those Isley's.

Love me deep and make it last,
I don't want this act of love to end fast.

You loved me good brought tears to my eyes,
loved me all night until the sun rise.

Then I started singing:
Ahh . Let's make love tonight,
Love me with all your might,
Please hold me tight.

I want every inch of your love;
you were sent to me from the heavens above.

It came to me like a big surprise,
the day you made me realize;

That I'm the one you love and I'm the one that's for ya,

I'm the one you need and that there's no otha.

I want to spend the rest of my life with you;

I want to be more than a wife to you.

Ahh, Let's make love tonight,
It was love at first sight,
Love me every night.
Ahh, Let's make love tonight!!!!!!!!!!!!!!!!!!!!!!!!!!!!!!!

HAVE ANYBODY SEEN MY MAN

He's very funny
Have plenty of money
And tells me I'm his only honey
He's always clean
To me he's never mean
And treats me like an African American Queen

HAVE ANYBODY SEEN MY MAN

He has a good job
Don't steal or rob
And when I put my hand on his Jones I can feel it throb
He don't think he's slick
My body he lick
And know how to work that nice size stick

HAVE ANYBODY SEEN MY MAN

He lets me know it's more than just lust
By his love upon me he thrust
My life to him I trust
He has the Midas touch
When I need him he's my crutch
And loves me oh, so, much

HAVE ANYBODY SEEN MY MAN

He's athletic
And very poetic
Makes me feel so energetic
And our physical attraction is magnetic
He's very clever
Supports me on whatever I endeavor
Says he loves me forever

EXCUSE ME, HAVE ANYBODY SEEN MY MAN

He don't see my independence as a threat
Our bodies close together dripping wet
Asks me if he can cum, I say, "not yet"
Knows how to keep me satisfied and that's a bet
Damn!!! Somebody pass me a cigarette
Or could it be possible we have not yet met

Will SOMEBODY ANSWER ME, HAVE ANYBODY SEEN MY MAN

Never once have he tried to scheme
He's a very good lover; he goes to the extreme
Filling me with ecstasy making me scream
Just the thought of him now is making me cream
He builds up my self-esteem
Tells me compared to others I'm supreme
Makes me feel like we're on the same team
But sometimes it seems
He's only in my dreams

PLEASE TELL ME, HAVE ANYBODY SEEN MY MAN

Sometimes life is so unfair
Because I know he's out there
I just don't know where
But when I find him true love we'll share
No other relationship would ever compare

RAISED IN THE GAME

They call me Sterling, Turks, ST or S
I've always lived my life with finesse
This is my story told hot off the press

At the time I had a strong mother there was no bother
Growing up in the 60s with no father

We had a small house no carpet, but it was clean
My Mom held it down she will always be my Queen

That young man you can't tame
He was Raised In The game

I took to heart what my momma said
Deep inside she knew I had to get my bread

She understood the situation
I had to lay down my own foundation

With her anxiety and frustration
I'm leaving Chi town with Milwaukee as my destination

Coming to stake my claim
I'm Raised In The Game

Uncle Tap took me under his wing
He cultivated me and showed me gambling was my thing

Tap taught me honor and integrity
That thugs are petty cowards with no sincerity

And never step over thousands to get to pennies my son
Have patience when hustling never jump the gun

He is a contributing factor to the man I became
I'm Raised In The Game

I am a product of my environment
The three boss player moves I had to represent

Gambling, pimping and selling pounds of weed
Getting paid I was going full speed
A good life for me was guaranteed

Everybody knows my name
I'm Raised In The Game

Queen Cocaine hits the streets
I had to get a piece of the sweets

Cash flowing hand over fist
Being crowned the King Pin I couldn't resist

Knowing that position came with a twist
And the dangers that followed exist

My empire I must proclaim
I'm Raised In The Game

I was polluting my community with drugs, gambling and racketeering
The State and the FBI was always interfering

Mayor and the police declared a war on drugs and crime
Coming down hard on the cities slime
Setting me up was just a matter of time

How they took me down was shame
I'm Raised In The Game

I am a man and take responsibility for what I've done
I must apologize to my mother, brothers, sisters, daughter and son

26 years in the belly of the beast
I was so far away from my family I felt I was in the Middle East
I meditated and kept my sanity at the least

In all those years they couldn't put out my flame
Because I'm Raised In The Game

The journey that cost me all those years
That brought me and my love ones to tears

I was broken down to my knees
I begged for forgiveness and for God to hear my pleas

I am now a changed man
My new life legacy has began
Starting over with a different plan

I'm at the bottom but the highest heights I aim
I'm Raised In The Game

I flood the streets with knowledge and my time I volunteer
My mission is very clear
To be a leader of the community frontier

I paid my dues and I did my time
I'm in my 60s and in my prime

I wanted out but I was addicted to the fame
It was only me to blame
It's my dignity for me to reclaim
I'm still Raised In The Game

Charge it to the Game

Some can't do me
That's just how it be

So I Charge It To The Game

When they step on my toes
God only knows

I Charge It To The Game

I make no assumptions
Due to I have the gumption

To Charge It To The Game

I take nothing personally
And will pray for you mercifully

And Charge It To The Game

Happy to be one of the best
Can pass the hustle test

Only to Charge It To The Game

Ready to proclaim
And never be shame
Of the hardship I overcame

Basically I Charge It To The Game

I wouldn't defame
My important name
For bright lights and fame

Charge It To The Game

Staying true to life I aim
Knowing when it's myself to blame
Not allowing others stump out my flame

I Will Charge It To The Game

Embracing the woman I've became
Letting all know I'm a feisty dame

That's Why I Charge It To The Game

AMUSEMENT PARK OF LIFE

Come on people; let's go to the AMUSEMENT PARK OF LIFE,
This park you'll always be the other woman never his wife,

Your heart will hurt as if you've been stabbed with a knife.
To your left is the VERY SCARY MERRY-GO-ROUND,
Where he'll make you feel the relationship is safe & sound,
There are plenty of bumps on the ride I've found.

It will take you up a high hill when you're feeling happy,
Because he just make sweet love to you, but, he always make it
snappy.

Then down a high hill when you're feeling depressed,
His love for you he confessed,
But, you know you're only second best.

Take a ride on the LOOP OF JEALOUSY.
Where the need to be with him is over-zealous, see.

Unknowingly you end up in the TUNNEL OF LONELINESS.
Where all you want is to be his one and only,
But instead of feeling alone, you now feel lonely.

Welcome to the HOUSE OF MIRRORS.
His intentions you wish he would make clearer,
And see he significant other as an interferer.

Then if you dare, enter the DUNGEON OF DESPAIR.
Where you're always feeling guilty about the affair,
Statistic states, for a man to leave his wife for the other woman is rare.

That woman I hate her, but, I don't know her, I have not a clue,
But then I realized she can't be that bad she have you.

Then you can take a dive in the DOSE OF REALITY,
Just the thought of him leaving her for you, he says is a fatality.
The words he says and the moves he make lack originality.

She don't have to work her bills he paid,
But all you get is promises and laid.

On holidays, he has to be the perfect daddy, husband and family man,
He will be nowhere in your plan and will sneak you a call if he can.

This ride is the scariest of them all,
It's called DENIAL HALL.

He's afraid she'll get half, because of the vow,
Because of the kids, he can't leave her now,
He tells you a divorce, she would never allow,
And for you to just wait, he'll get out of it somehow.

But ladies all he wants is his cake and to eat it too.
So remove yourself from the situation, because the end results, he's not choosing you.

DIVA

A DIVA is what I am, D.I.V.A
Dauntless, Idealistic, Valorous, Accomplished

Internationally known, all across the U.S.A. I've flown,
And praise the fact I have a mind of my own

A DIVA is what I am, D.I.V.A
Dashing, Intelligent, Vibrant, Artistic

I strive to be, the perfect mother you see, that's why everyone agree,
that a good life for me, is a guarantee.

A DIVA is what I am, D.I.V.A
Debonair, Independent, Versatile, Admired

For my money I work hard,
from imitators to player haters I must be on guard,
Because I have a little more in my backyard.

A DIVA is what I am, D.I V.A
Dignified, Invincible, Voluptuous, Alluring

This ass so tight, MEN, I'll serve it to you like rump roast at a deli,
With a rap so smooth your minds will turn to jelly,
Even when I'm not around, just the thought of me gives you
butterflies in your belly.

A DIVA is what I am, D.I.V.A
Deserving, Intimidating, Valuable, Amazing

Gold rings with big rocks,
Plenty of money I clocks,
The secret to being a DIVA I unlocks,
Do you have to ask why they call me the Phox?

A DIVA is what I am, D.I.V.A
Dependable, Interesting, Viable, Affectionate

So I say this to you up & coming DIVAS.
This may sound a little bold,
And It might come off as being cold,
Listen, I'm not here to scold,
But, girlfriends don't ever let your world be controlled,
And always remember true game is to be sold not told.

A DIVA IS WHAT WE ARE

GHETTO BOUGIE

GO FOR THE MILLIONS I WAS TAUGHT
I MADE IT MORE THAN A MERE THOUGHT
TO HAVE ME IN YOUR LIFE IS AN AFFIRMATIVE HONEY
I STRAIGHT UP HELP OTHERS MAKE THEIR MONEY
FINE AND STRONG WITH A VIRTUOUS BRAIN
I'M BOLD ENOUGH TO JUMP OUT OF AN AIRPLANE

FOLKS MAY AGREE
I'M GHETTO BOUGIE

I'VE BEEN ON LET'S MAKE A DEAL AND WON PRIZES
AT MY MATURE AGE I NOW UNDERSTAND COMPROMISES
I'VE TRAVELLED AND I'M INTERNATIONALLY KNOWN
ALL OVER THE WORLD I'VE FLOWN
DRINKING $100 BOTTLES OF DON PERIGNON CHAMPAGNE
I'M FANCY AND HAVE STYLE MY WARDROBE IS OFF THE
CHAIN

I'M ALWAYS AUTHENTIC AND CAREFREE
I'M GHETTO BOUGIE

I COULD NEVER APPEAR DISROBED I AM FAR TOO INHIBITED
HOWEVER I WILL SHOW MY ASS COMPLIMENTARY TO
NERVES UNLIMITED
I'M A BLACKBELT AND CAN KARATE CHOP YOU IN THE
THROAT
I LOVE POEMS AND THIS IS JUST A LITTLE SOMETHING
ABOUT ME I WROTE
I'VE CAME UP AFTER HITTING THE NOTORIOUS SKIDS
I'M ALSO A FUNDRAISER AND MAKE THAT CASH FLOW FOR
THE KIDS

I WILL TOAST TO YOU WITH A GLASS FULL OF WHITE CHABLIS
I'M GHETTO BOUGIE

MY CRIMES AND DECEITFULNESS HAS BEEN FORGOTTEN
MY MAN LOVE ME TO THE CORE AND SPOILS ME ROTTEN
IN MY LIFE OF HUSTLE THERE WERE DAYS I THOUGHT I WAS
A GONER
HAPPY TO HAVE THAT NICE CRIB IN THE HOOD ON THE
CORNER
IN THIS PIECE I'M TELLING YOU WHAT I'M ALL ABOUT
I'M SEXY AND UNAPOLOGETICALLY ALWAYS BRINGING IT OUT

EVERY NOW AND THEN A SHOPPING SPREE
I WILL PROUDLY WEAR THE LABEL OF BEING GHETTO
BOUGIE

BLACK & GOLD

Dasha at the MECCA must have a man,
I'm sure together they have a lifelong plan.
I'm thinking Dasha must have a good man,
telling her she can do it, yes she can.
You see, Dasha can see in her man true happiness,
his love for her he must express.
This is only my guess.
She has a body at night to keep her warm,
When she wants to get down, he ready to perform.
She have a man to pay half her bill maybe all,
takes her on trips and shopping at the mall.
Yeah, she found her BLACK & GOLD,
The beauty of her relationship is to behold,
But now it's time to let the true story unfold.
Thursday she stood there talked about me right in my face,
Like being man less is a disgrace,
Girlfriend I'm here to tell you that isn't the case.
Dasha, I can't deal with a man working for $5 an hour and have no willpower.
I can't deal with thugs that drinks plenty, sell or use heavy drugs.
I can't deal with unnecessary lies,
saying anything to get between my thighs.
I can't deal with a man that gambles his money away,

If he sees a short skirt and big breast, he'll stray
and tells me his orders I must obey.
I can't deal with the little babies and the baby mama drama,
Or my mind going through the trauma.
I can't deal with the cheating on me and his wife,
He only has time for his friends and the nightlife.
I can't afford to deal with the mental, physical, psychological and
emotional abuse,
Trying to communicate with him is no use.
I looked up and down Hampton for the BLACK & GOLD,
All I find is the streets are cold,
And it's a very bumpy road.
I can't deal with the jealousy or in his mind I think I'm slick,
His momma and everybody know he's a lunatic.
I can't deal with the Motha Fucka telling me if leave him he'll kill me,
I refuse to deal with that shit in 2003.
I can't deal with the obsessive and the possessiveness one man can
bring,
No desire to take thing further or give me a ring.
I can't deal with a nigga who's 40, don't know how to keep a job,
FEDS after him and his mob.

I can't deal with a man that thinks "MY CAR" is "OUR CAR" even if he's never paid not one car note,
not sure of himself, always a scapegoat.
I can't deal with bad breath, funky feet and a stanking ass,
Don't know how to dress and have no class.
I swear I looked high and low for the BLACK & GOLD.
All I found is the streets are icy cold,
And it's a very, very bumpy road.
I can't deal with a nigga that thinks PHOXXY have 3 jobs; she should help me out,
When it comes to good men it's definitely a drought.
I can't deal with the man that can't handle commitment,
Disappears for days when it's time to pay the rent.
I can't deal with a man that don't know slavery is illegal,
Wants me to treat him as if he's regal.
I can't deal with the man that's institutionalized and can't stay on the streets long,
I shouldn't have to deal with that bullshit, right of wrong?
I can't deal with the male chauvinist pig,
Strutting with his chest out like he's a bigwig.
To be honest I search hard for the BLACK & GOLD,
But, half the brothers I know just got paroled,
So, Dasha after making your man did God break the mold?

AIN'T NOTHING NICE

You've tried dipping in my business for the longest,
ever since you discovered my game was the strongest.

I'm in the life, but, not in the game,
don't your punk ass realize the two-isn't the same.

I'm going to show you bitch you don't have to think twice,
PHOXXY, ain't nothing nice.

You think you got over and played me for a sucker,
let me tell you one thing you lousy Mother Fucker.

I'm true to the life, the life been true to me,
that punk shit you pulled won't affect my cash flow see.

So Nigga, you must pay the price to find out that PHOXXY ain't
nothing nice.

You know fully well I'm a female player from the old school,
I grew up not crossing your homey as a rule.

You will find out sooner or later,
that this bad attitude I have you're the creator,
and comparing us two you know I am greater.

All I want you to do is take my advice,
before you find out the hard way that PHOXXY ain't nothing nice.

I got knives in my back I didn't know who it was,
I found out it was my Guy with some help from my Cuz.

Blood is thicker than mud they say,
he must be playing hooky when they taught the lesson that day.

I hate to make this sacrifice,
I have no choice but to show him that PHOXXY ain't nothing nice.

The moves you make you thought was down,
I took it like a player without a frown,
and I am not going to show my ass or clown.

Because, whether you're a pimp, player, prostitute, hoe, heifer or hustler I don't mind,
because, being down comes in all kinds,
and I'll be with you 100% if you're real you'll find.

It's not about the games you play it's how you play it,
that sneaking and conniving behind one's back ain't about shit.

So I must be precise,
in my telling you, you ain't nothing nice.

The player etiquette handbook is what you need,
because I don't understand this new breed,
stepping on ones toes for your own selfish needs.

Just like snake eyes at the roll of the dice,
if you fit any one of these descriptions you know for a fact your ass
ain't nothing nice.

You know I taught you half the things you know boy, now you're
playing with my intellect as if it was a toy
.
I know you know because I showed your ass,
how to hustle with finesse and class.

The likes of you, out my world I must ice,
cause fake ass nigga you ain't nothing nice.

Now you're walking around with your chest out thinking you've
played me,
that's going to cost your jive ass that times three.

So sit back and take this pencil whooping like a man, stop your
tripping if you can,
before I make some shit hit the fan.

Just like nasty ass roaches and mice,
the shit that you put down ain't nothing nice.

Now you got your cool points taken away Joe.
Because I gave you that action don't you know?

Sooner or later you will understand precisely.
Why the PHOX took the whole situation so nicely.

YOU AIN'T NOTHING NICE!!!

THIS MONSTER CALLED CANCER

UNEXPLAINED WEIGHT LOSS OR WEIGHT GAIN

SYMPTOMS LIKE CRAMPS, BLOATING AND GAS PAIN

MANY NOTICABLE CHANGES WITHOUT AN ANSWER

THIS MONSTER CALLED CANCER

CHANGES IN APPETITE, NAUSEA AND VOMITING

AFRAID TO ADMIT THEIR DISEASE COMMITING

DIMINISHING YOUR WHOLE TROOP AND YOUR DANCER

THIS MONSTER CALLED CANCER

SHORTNESS OF BREATH, WHEEZING AND HEADACHES

GIVEN MONTHS TO LIVE MAKE YOUR HEART BREAKS

A LONG WAY FROM A MODERN DAY ROMANCER

THIS MONSTER CALLED CANCER

MOLES CHANGING THEIR COLOR AND SIZE

AT NIGHT I OFTEN HEAR YOUR CRIES

OPERATIONS, CHEMOTHERAPY AND A BIG LANCER

THIS MONSTER CALLED CANCER

FEVERS, CHILLS AND LYMPH NODE SWELLING

MOANS OF I'M TIRED YOU'RE YELLING

INFECTING YOUR BODY LIKE PSYCHOTIC PRANCER

THIS MONSTER CALLED CANCER

PRAYING TO THE UNIVERSE PLEASE TAKE THE PAIN AWAY

IN HEAVEN WE'LL MEET ANOTHER DAY

NEEDING A SPIRITUAL ADVISER AND AN
EMOTIONAL ENHANCER

THIS MONSTER CALLED CANCER

26 MINUTES

I HAVE 26 MINUTES TO DO THIS POEM

I WISH IT WAS 26 MINUTES BEFORE GOING HOME

IN 26 MINUTES WHAT CAN ONE DO

I'M BORED SO I'll LIST A FEW THINGS FOR YOU

IN 26 MINUTES YOU CAN GO TO LUNCH

I'M NOT SURE WHAT THEY DO IN 26 MINUTES BUT I HAVE A HUNCH

*IN 26 MINUTES YOU CAN CLEAN OUT YOUR DESK
OR CLEAN YOUR HOUSE*

YOU MAY HAVE TIME FOR YOUR MAN IF HE BECOMES AROUSED

IN 26 MINUTES YOU CAN MAKE LOVE A COUPLE OF TIMES

OR BE LIKE US FIVE WOMEN AND BUST OUT SOME SILLY RHYMES

IT'S BITTERSWEET

My days are filled with deep thoughts of you

My mouth waters with the worst fears I can't undo

Pain so deep it cuts like a knife

Sometimes it don't seems like real life

Trying to mend the broken, scattered pieces you left on my heart

Like all hopes to soon depart

This is where grief, life, joy, and sorrow meet

Is this the glorious destination that drove you...Damn...It's bittersweet

They say time heals all wounds somehow I don't believe this much is true

After all those years happiness was far in between and few

You lied to cover up your deceitful ways

I was too naïve to question your plays

So sad and with so wild a start

You were the artist and I was your art

I was so complete

Or so I thought…Damn…It's bittersweet

I pretend that you don't still drive me wild

Your spell had me acting like a helpless child

Hoping that you will call my name as you pass by

I want to be yours…my...oh…my

I need you to make me whole again

Meet me where it all began

Life is funny here we go again

Damn…how do I really know if it's bitter or sweet
then…

(This poem was co-written by Louria Jewett)

Thank you "WIFE"

AIN'T NOTHING NICE

Made in the USA
San Bernardino, CA
11 January 2020